This Jou

with Love by:

_____

(Awesome Son)

AND

_____

(Awesome Mom)

Mom's
Age

Son's
Age

_____

Date Journal Started

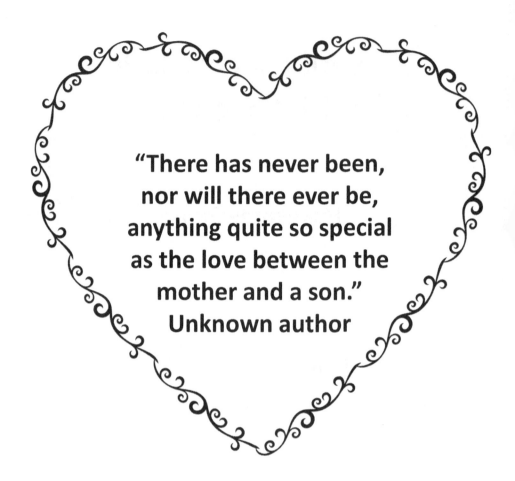

"There has never been,
nor will there ever be,
anything quite so special
as the love between the
mother and a son."
Unknown author

How to Use This Journal:

I am a mom of two children – a girl and a boy. While my daughter is more vocal, my teenage son doesn't show as much emotion and it is not always easy to find out what is going on in his mind & life.

If you are a mom to a tween or a teenage boy like me, and you'd like to open up the lines of communication, this journal is a safe and fun way to do it.

This journal is filled with questions or prompts. You don't have to answer them in any particular order. You can work on the journal together, or you can take turns with the journal, and then agree upon a location to place the journal when you are each done writing your answers so that the responses can be read privately.

How to Use This Journal:

The journal is set up so that, in most cases, the son and mom answer similar questions on the same page. At the end of the journal, there are some extra pages where only mom or son answer. In addition, you can create your own questions that one or both of you may want answered.

There are a few pages that are purposely left blank so you can choose to add what you want – photos, hand drawings, doodles, space to write more, etc.

Take your time and enjoy the journey of getting to know one another better!

"Sons are the anchors of a mother's life."
Sophocles

I know my mom loves me, because she ....

_____

_____

_____

_____

_____

I know my son loves me, because he....

_____

_____

_____

_____

_____

Son, what are 3 things that make you happy?

_____

_____

_____

_____

Mom, what are 3 things that make you happy?

_____

_____

_____

_____

Son, what are 3 things that make you sad?

_____

_____

_____

_____

Mom, what are 3 things that make you sad?

_____

_____

_____

_____

Son, what are 3 things that make you angry?

_____

_____

_____

_____

_____

Mom, what are 3 things that make you angry?

_____

_____

_____

_____

_____

Son, what do you like most about yourself?

_____

_____

_____

_____

_____

Mom, what do you like most about yourself?

_____

_____

_____

_____

_____

Son, is there anything that you would like to change about yourself? Why?

_____

_____

_____

_____

_____

Mom, is there anything that you would like to change about yourself? Why?

_____

_____

_____

_____

_____

Son, what are your two favorite colors? How about your least favorite colors?

_____

_____

_____

_____

_____

Mom, what are your two favorite colors? How about your least favorite colors?

_____

_____

_____

_____

_____

Son, what are your favorite foods?   Your Least favorite foods?

_____

_____

_____

_____

_____

Mom, what are your favorite foods? Your least favorite foods?

_____

_____

_____

_____

_____

Son, what are your three favorite subjects at school?

_____

_____

_____

_____

Mom, what were your three favorite subjects when you went to school?

_____

_____

_____

_____

_____

Son, what are your three LEAST favorite subjects at school?

_____

_____

_____

_____

_____

Mom, what were your three LEAST favorite subjects when you went to school?

_____

_____

_____

_____

_____

Son, when you wake up, what do you look most forwards to doing in a day?

_____

_____

_____

_____

_____

Mom, when you wake up, what do you look most forwards to doing in a day?

_____

_____

_____

_____

_____

Son, when you are living on your own one day, do you want pets? If so, what kind? Do you have ideas of names for them?

_____

_____

_____

_____

_____

Mom, have you had any pets growing up, and what were their names?

_____

_____

_____

_____

"All that I am, or I hope to be, I owe to my angel mother."
Abraham Lincoln

Son, who is your favorite teacher and why?

_____

_____

_____

_____

_____

Mom, did you have any favorite teachers and why were they your favorites?

_____

_____

_____

_____

_____

Son, have you ever or are you now being bullied?

_____

_____

_____

_____

_____

Mom, were you ever bullied as a kid, and if so, what did you do about it?

_____

_____

_____

_____

_____

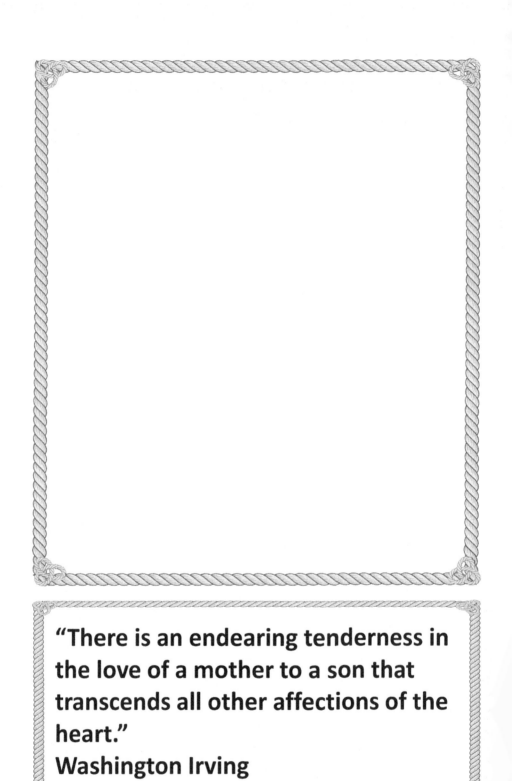

"There is an endearing tenderness in the love of a mother to a son that transcends all other affections of the heart."
Washington Irving

Son, what are the names of your friends?

_____

_____

_____

_____

_____

Mom, who were your friends when you were growing up?

_____

_____

_____

_____

_____

Son, what do you appreciate the most about your friends?

_____

_____

_____

_____

_____

Mom, what do you appreciate most about your friends?

_____

_____

_____

_____

_____

Son, if you could have one superpower, what would it be?

_____

_____

_____

_____

_____

Mom, if you could have one superpower, what would it be?

_____

_____

_____

_____

_____

Son, what do you find is the hardest thing about being a kid?

_____

_____

_____

_____

_____

Mom, what did you find was the hardest thing about being a kid?

_____

_____

_____

_____

_____

Son, what do you find is the easiest thing about being a kid?

_____

_____

_____

_____

_____

Mom, what do you find was the easiest thing about being a kid?

_____

_____

_____

_____

_____

Son, do you have any teenage crushes?

_____

_____

_____

_____

_____

Mom, did you have any teenage crushes when you were growing up?

_____

_____

_____

_____

_____

Son, what would you like to do when you grow up?

_____

_____

_____

_____

_____

Mom, what kinds of occupations did you consider when you were younger?

_____

_____

_____

_____

_____

Son, what concerns you the most about living on your own?

_____

_____

_____

_____

_____

Mom, what concerned you the most about living on your own?

_____

_____

_____

_____

_____

Son, are you excited or fearful about going to college or university and why?

_____

_____

_____

_____

_____

Mom, were you excited or scared about going to college or university?

_____

_____

_____

_____

_____

Son, what is something mom always say to you that you like (even though you may not show it)?

_____

_____

_____

_____

_____

Mom, what is something that your son says that you like?

_____

_____

_____

_____

_____

Son, what new things are you learning at school right now, and what do you find most interesting?

_____

_____

_____

_____

_____

Mom, what things did you find most interesting to learn at school?

_____

_____

_____

_____

_____

Son, if you could meet one famous person, who would it be? Why?

_____

_____

_____

_____

_____

Mom, if you could meet one famous person, who would it be? Why?

_____

_____

_____

_____

_____

Son, is there something(s) that mom does or says that you don't like?

_____

_____

_____

_____

_____

Mom, is there anything your son says or does that you don't like?

_____

_____

_____

_____

_____

Son, what hurts your feelings?

_____

_____

_____

_____

_____

Mom, what hurts your feelings?

_____

_____

_____

_____

_____

Son, what do you think are 6 words that describe your mom best?

_____

_____

_____

_____

_____

Mom, what do you think are 6 words that describe your son best?

_____

_____

_____

_____

_____

Son, what do you think are 6 words that describe you best?

_____

_____

_____

_____

_____

Mom, what do you think are 6 words that describe you best?

_____

_____

_____

_____

_____

Son, is there something mom knows how to do, that you would like her to teach you?

_____

_____

_____

_____

_____

Mom, is there something that your son knows how to do that you would like him to teach you?

_____

_____

_____

_____

_____

Son, what are three things that you would have a hard time living without?

_____

_____

_____

_____

_____

Mom, what are three things that you would have a hard time living without?

_____

_____

_____

_____

_____

Son, what are your favorite restaurants (list them as #1. being your most favorite)?

_____

_____

_____

_____

_____

Mom, what are your favorite restaurants (list #1. as your favorite and so on)?

_____

_____

_____

_____

_____

Son, what is something that we've never done that you would like to do together?

_____

_____

_____

_____

_____

Mom, what is something that we've never done that you would like to do together?

_____

_____

_____

_____

_____

Son, what are your favorite sports teams?

_____

_____

_____

_____

_____

Mom, what are your favorite sports teams?

_____

_____

_____

_____

_____

Son, what are your favorite card or boardgames?

_____

_____

_____

_____

_____

Mom, what are your favorite card or boardgames?

_____

_____

_____

_____

_____

Son, what are your favorite video games?

_____

_____

_____

_____

_____

Mom, what video games have you played before?

_____

_____

_____

_____

_____

Son, what kind of music do you like the most and least?

_____

_____

_____

_____

_____

Mom, what kind of music do you like the most and least?

_____

_____

_____

_____

_____

Son, who exactly are your favorite musicians, musical groups, or songs?

_____

_____

_____

_____

_____

Mom, who exactly are your favorite musicians, musical groups, or songs?

_____

_____

_____

_____

_____

_____

Son, how do you like to show people that you care about them?

_____

_____

_____

_____

_____

Mom, how do you like to show people that you care about them?

_____

_____

_____

_____

_____

"There is an endearing tenderness in the love of a mother to a son that transcends all other affections of the heart."
Washington Irving

Son, in descending order of importance, what are your favorite sports to participate in?

_____

_____

_____

_____

_____

Mom, in descending order of importance, what are your favorite sports to participate in?

_____

_____

_____

_____

_____

Son, what instruments or sports would you be interested in trying in the future?

_____

_____

_____

_____

_____

Mom, what instruments or sports would you be interested in trying?

_____

_____

_____

_____

_____

Son, what do you think your mom does at her job?

_____

_____

_____

_____

_____

Mom, what subjects is your son taking in school right now?

_____

_____

_____

_____

_____

Son, if you won a million dollars, what would you do with it?

_____

_____

_____

_____

_____

Mom, if you won a million dollars, what would you do with it?

_____

_____

_____

_____

_____

Son, what are you most proud of accomplishing in life so far?

_____

_____

_____

_____

_____

Mom, which accomplishments are you most proud of?

_____

_____

_____

_____

_____

Son, what is one thing that you have done that you are not proud of?

_____

_____

_____

_____

_____

Mom, what is one thing that you have done that you are not proud of?

_____

_____

_____

_____

_____

Son, what do you do at lunch break/recess breaks at school?

_____

_____

_____

_____

_____

Mom, what do you do at lunch break or coffee breaks at your work?

_____

_____

_____

_____

_____

Son, what do you feel are things that you are really good at?

_____

_____

_____

_____

_____

Mom, what are things that you feel that you are really good at?

_____

_____

_____

_____

_____

Son, no one is good at everything. What things are you not good at?

_____

_____

_____

_____

_____

Mom, what are things that you are not good at?

_____

_____

_____

_____

_____

Son, if you could be invisible for one day, what would you do?

_____

_____

_____

_____

Mom, if you could be invisible for one day, what would you do?

_____

_____

_____

_____

_____

Son, if you could be one Superhero, who would you be?

_____

_____

_____

_____

_____

Mom, if you could be one Superhero, who would you be?

_____

_____

_____

_____

_____

Son, what do you think makes people happy in life?

_____

_____

_____

_____

_____

Mom, what do you think makes people happy in life?

_____

_____

_____

_____

_____

Son, do you think you want to get married and have a family in the future?

_____

_____

_____

_____

Mom, what made you decide to have a family?

_____

_____

_____

_____

_____

Son, what are you most thankful/grateful for?

_____

_____

_____

_____

_____

Mom, what are you most thankful/grateful for?

_____

_____

_____

_____

_____

Son, who are your favorite and least favorite teachers and why?

_____

_____

_____

_____

_____

Mom, who were your favorite and least favorite teachers and why?

_____

_____

_____

_____

_____

Son, can you think of something that your mom has said or done that was funny?

_____

_____

_____

_____

_____

Mom, what has your son said or done that you thought was funny?

_____

_____

_____

_____

_____

Son, what are your most favorite and least favorite seasons and why?

_____

_____

_____

_____

_____

Mom, what are your most favorite and less favorite seasons and why?

_____

_____

_____

_____

_____

Son, what is your favorite holiday? What is your next favorite holiday and so forth?

_____

_____

_____

_____

_____

Mom, what are your favorite holidays, in descending order?

_____

_____

_____

_____

_____

Son, of all the things you have learned so far in life, what do you think will help you the most as an adult?

_____

_____

_____

_____

_____

Mom, what things did you learn when you were younger that helped you most as an adult?

_____

_____

_____

_____

_____

Son, if you could travel back in time, what is one piece of technology of today that you would take with you? Why?

_____

_____

_____

_____

_____

Mom, what is one piece of technology that you would take with you if you traveled back in time? Why?

_____

_____

_____

_____

_____

Son, if you could travel back in time to 3 years ago, what would you tell your younger self?

_____

_____

_____

_____

_____

Mom, if you could travel back in time to 3 years ago, what would you tell your younger self?

_____

_____

_____

_____

_____

Son, if you could be famous, what would you want to be famous for?

_____

_____

_____

_____

_____

Mom, if you would be famous, what would you want to be famous for?

_____

_____

_____

_____

_____

Son, what could you do to make the world a better place?

_____

_____

_____

_____

_____

Mom, what have you done or could you do to make the world a better place?

_____

_____

_____

_____

_____

Son, if you could do some volunteer work, what would you choose?

_____

_____

_____

_____

_____

Mom, what kind of volunteer work have you done or would you like to do?

_____

_____

_____

_____

_____

Son, if you could learn a new language, what would it be?

_____

_____

_____

_____

_____

Mom, if you could learn a new language, what would it be?

_____

_____

_____

_____

_____

Son, what things do you like most/appreciate about the country we live in?

_____

_____

_____

_____

_____

Mom, what things do you like most/appreciate about the country we live in?

_____

_____

_____

_____

_____

"A man loves his sweetheart the most, his wife the best, but his mother the longest."
Irish Proverb

Son, what pieces of technology do you think your mom liked and used most when she was growing up?

_____

_____

_____

_____

Mom, what pieces of technology did you use when you were growing up?

_____

_____

_____

_____

_____

Son, if you could make the rules for at home, what would they be?

_____

_____

_____

_____

_____

Mom, were there any rules that you did not like when you were growing up?

_____

_____

_____

_____

_____

Son, if you could be President or Prime Minister for one day, what would you do?

_____

_____

_____

_____

_____

Mom, if you could be President or Prime Minister for one day, what would you do?

_____

_____

_____

_____

_____

Son, if you could spend one whole day with mom, what would you want to do to make it the perfect day?

_____

_____

_____

_____

_____

Mom, if you could spend one whole day with your son, what would you want to do to make it the perfect day?

_____

_____

_____

_____

_____

Son, what is your favorite thing about living at home? And what is your least favorite?

_____

_____

_____

_____

_____

Mom, what was your favorite thing about living at home? And what was your least favorite?

_____

_____

_____

_____

_____

Son, do you think teens today have it easier or harder than mom did? Why?

_____

_____

_____

_____

_____

Mom, do you think teens today have it easier or harder than when you were growing up? Why?

_____

_____

_____

_____

_____

Son, what makes you believe that a Higher Being exists?

_____

_____

_____

_____

_____

Mom, what makes you believe that a Higher Being exists?

_____

_____

_____

_____

_____

Son, are you satisfied with the number of friends you have, and the quality of your friendships?

_____

_____

_____

_____

_____

Mom, are you satisfied with the number of friends you have, and the quality of your friendships?

_____

_____

_____

_____

_____

Son, what things can your mom do to make you feel more supported?

_____

_____

_____

_____

_____

Mom, are there things that your son can do to help you out more?

_____

_____

_____

_____

_____

Son, what do you think it means to achieve success in life?

_____

_____

_____

_____

_____

Mom, what do you think success in life involves?

_____

_____

_____

_____

_____

Son, do you think your mom treats you and your sibling(s) fairly?

_____

_____

_____

_____

_____

Mom, do you think your mother treats/treated you and your sibling(s) fairly?

_____

_____

_____

_____

_____

Mom, what are your memories of your pregnancy with your son?

_____

_____

_____

_____

_____

_____

_____

_____

_____

_____

_____

_____

_____

_____

_____

_____

Mom, tell your son about the day he was born.

_____

_____

_____

_____

_____

_____

_____

_____

_____

_____

_____

_____

_____

_____

_____

_____

Mom, tell your son things that you did together when he was a baby, toddler, & preschooler that he may not recall.

_____

_____

_____

_____

_____

_____

_____

_____

_____

_____

_____

_____

_____

_____

_____

_____

_____

Son, tell me a story about what went on at school this week.

_____

_____

_____

_____

_____

_____

_____

_____

_____

_____

_____

_____

_____

_____

_____

_____

Son, what are your FAVORITE 3 memories (Describe something we did, or somewhere we went)?

_____

_____

_____

_____

_____

_____

_____

_____

_____

_____

_____

_____

_____

_____

_____

_____

_____

Mom, describe some of your earliest memories in life.

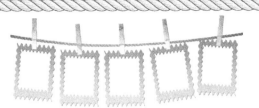

Post a photo here
of mother and son.

"Happy is the son whose faith in his mother remains unchallenged."
Louisa May Alcott

Son, which of mom's recipes would you like for her to print for you below?

_____

_____

_____

_____

_____

_____

_____

_____

_____

_____

_____

_____

_____

_____

_____

_____

_____

"My mother is my root, my foundation. She planted the seed that I base my life on, and that is the belief that the ability to achieve starts in your mind." – Michael Jordan

"I'll love you forever, I'll like you for always, as long as I'm living my baby you'll be."
Robert Munsch

Date Journal Completed:

_____

Made in the USA
Columbia, SC
09 March 2024

32902944R00068